KIMBERLY QUARTEY

Empath
AND
Psychic
abilities

The Complete Survival Guide for Highly Sensitive People.
Develop Supernatural Powers Such as Intuition
and Clairvoyance with Guided Meditations

KIMBERLY QUARTEY

Table of Contents

Introduction

I want to ask you something, have you met people who seemed to know how you felt before saying something? Or, I ask you in another way, have you felt how other people feel even though their body and verbal language don't express it? You may be a psychic empath, a person deeply in tune with the needs of others. Although everyone can access their psychic side, some people seem to have a special gift for reading the needs of another and seeing beyond what meets our mortal eyes.

This book is about that. It is aimed at people who have that gift and use it or still don't know how to use it. Empathy is the ability to read the emotions of others without them saying it. Thoughts and feelings are understood, and aura reading comes into play—how to read it and learn to feel the energy around it. The psychic empath tends to carry the emotional baggage of others. They may find themselves regularly exhausted and in need of learning basic protective skills so that they do not absorb the energies of others.

They have great empathy and mental capacity. Psychics can use their abilities to detect subtle energy changes. This makes them especially gifted in reiki, crystal healing, and other forms of healing where energy plays a key role. Advanced psychics can even see auras and tell which chakras are blocked. Their clairvoyance makes them very talented as spiritual advisors, and they can build careers among psychics. Most people who practice psychological empathy tend toward a career as a counselor or spiritual therapist. You can even find them working as doctors, nurses, and therapists, where they can make the most of their skills.

Throughout the pages, you will know what empathy is, the aura, how to improve psychic abilities, understand empaths, and understand yourself. You will learn to heal, protect your energy, and improve relationships with others by getting to know yourself better.

Chapter 1
Psychic Abilities—A Mystery Beyond the Senses

Understanding this wonderful world that is before our eyes but that we sometimes do not see or refuse to recognize implies that we begin by understanding a series of basic concepts about psychic abilities, such as telepathy, auras and their readings, and clairvoyance. In this first chapter, I will talk about it.

The Art of Clairvoyant Reading and Healing

The word seer refers to people with the extrasensory capacity of clairvoyance, which allows them to reveal uncertainty and see beyond what others can. Although the word refers to someone who perceives the world through vision, the meaning is broader when it comes to psychics who have the gift of clairvoyance. The gift of clairvoyance allows the enlightened person to see beyond. This encompasses not just the perception of sight or images but also sounds and experiences, information or knowledge hidden from most people.

Clairvoyant Telepathy

Although communication between beings improves every day, which will bear fruit, there is still a shell between beings that limits the connection. The soul is invisible and impenetrable if we want it that way. We look at ourselves, we see ourselves externally, and we communicate with our bodies, with our eyes, and with oral signs and written language, but we do not see the interior of people. We are almost always unaware of each person's intention and authentic essence. A trajectory can indeed be observed in each person that is usually revealing the reality of each individual, but it is necessary to wait a long time to be able to assess it. Sometimes after their death, something not so uncommon.

From the body message to the visual, the oral, the written, the network... what will be the next one? I want to dream that it will be the mental connector, the telepathic language. The mind can transmit and receive "wireless." Perhaps we are still in the initial stage, but I know that this is so and that we have to develop the necessary capacities to make telepathy between beings possible. Who has not experienced situations in which it is not necessary to speak, and we are allowed to transmit our thoughts and read the minds of others with ease? It is true that it only happens in certain circumstances, but it could be the beginning of a new learning process. Like the smell, minds develop one more sense to read thoughts, and these pass between them. Sharing them is already a privilege. The mental message would suppose a whole world of connection that has to arrive. And while it arrives, how can we not perceive the slight degree that we already have? I experience many situations that make it tangible to me, and I would say that daily practice enhances the capacity, like languages.

For its part, clairvoyant telepathy is an ability that only a select few possess, a blessing they received the moment they arrived in this world. Clairvoyance is the ability to understand people's past, present, and future through images. While there are still many who do not believe those who claim to master this art of divination, more and more people are beginning to succumb to the masters' talents, and they are proving that clairvoyance has real power.

With the rapid development of technology, more and more women are dedicating themselves to this beautiful profession. The Internet has become the perfect medium through which many experts can showcase their talents and allow people to experience their skills.

What Is Telepathy?

Telepathy is the ability to communicate thoughts and/or ideas through means other than the five senses we learn about in school: seeing, hearing, smelling, tasting, and touching. Telepathy is a way of communicating with another person. One person may be thinking or sending a thought to another, and the other person may receive or feel the same thought. This explains why when you randomly think of your best friend from college, they text you the next day. Or that time you accidentally called your cousin, and she said, "Oh my gosh, I was thinking of you!"

Types of Telepathy

Our etheric body is part of the ocean of interactive energy that connects us to everyone and everything in the world. It is through it that we send and receive telepathic messages.

Instinctive Telepathy

Instinctive telepathy is the most common type of telepathy. We share this type of telepathy with the animal kingdom, and it remains a prevalent mode of communication in indigenous cultures. Instinctive telepathy uses the area around the solar plexus, the center of instinct and emotion.

In this type of telepathy, a person registers the feelings or needs of another at a distance. These tests can be found in a wide variety of cultures, both ancient and modern. In every culture, the area around the solar plexus is key. According to the *kahunas*, one person's *akā* or etheric body sends a "finger" or thread of *akā* matter to another person's solar plexus. The connection is made, and the messages are sent.

Animal Telepathy

Instinctive telepathy is in animals. Collective telepathy, the most common form of instinctual telepathy, can be seen in the mysterious migration patterns of birds, fish, insects, and other animals. The power of dogs and other animals to know when their owners are coming back is one that we possess and makes us connect with other beings in a way that, without knowing this theory, is inexplicable.

Mental Telepathy

Mental telepathy, or mind transfer, is mind-to-mind telepathy. It makes use of the throat center and the lower levels of the psychic plane. Being able to practice it requires focused and unidirectional attention. Unlike hypnotic channeling, which is a means whereby a disembodied entity uses the psychic's body to communicate a message, telepathic contact takes place between two conscious, focused minds.

Spiritual Telepathy

Spiritual or soul-to-soul telepathy is the highest type of telepathy. It uses the higher levels of the spiritual plane. Spiritual telepathy is only possible when we create a connection between the brain, mind, and soul. When we tune in to our brain, mind, and soul, we can act as intermediaries between the physical and spiritual worlds.

Steps to Develop Telepathy

These are the steps to follow to develop telepathy:

1. **Tune in to your bodily senses.** Try playing white noise through headphones and wear protective glasses. Shifting your attention away from your physical sensations allows you to focus more deeply on sending telepathic messages.

2. **Stretch your muscles or try yoga.** Trying to send a telepathic message requires a lot of mental concentration, so try to relax as much as possible. Regular stretching and yoga practice can help you learn how to achieve a state of relaxation and focus.

3. **Meditate to calm your mind.** Wear loose clothing and sit upright in a comfortable posture. Breathe in and out slowly, doing your best to clear your mind of unwanted thoughts. Imagine that as you exhale, scattered and random thoughts go through your mind.

4. **View the person who receives the message.** Close your eyes and visualize the receiver as clearly as possible. Try to imagine them sitting or standing in front of you. See the details in your mind, such as the person's eye color, weight, height, hair length, and the way they sit or stand.

5. **Imagine what it's like to connect with people.** Remember how you felt when you met this person face to face. Feel these emotions as if the person were actually in front of you. Focus on these feelings and trust that you are connecting with others.

6. **Focus on a single image or word.** When you're just starting, stick to something simple, like nearby objects. Visualize it in as much detail as possible and focus your attention on it. Focus on how it looks, how it feels to the touch, and how it makes you feel.

7. **Send your message.** After forming a clear mental image, imagine the object moving from your mind to the recipient's mind. Imagine yourself face to face with the recipient and say "apple" or whatever thought you are conveying. In your mind's eye, see the accomplishment on their faces when they understand what you are saying.

8. **Ask the recipient to write down anything that comes to mind.** Once you have sent the message, the recipient should remain relaxed and

open until they feel a thought enter their head. Then they have to write whatever comes to mind.

9. **Compare the results with each other.** When you're both ready, you and the recipient should show each other what you've written. Don't get discouraged if you don't succeed, especially at first. Take a moment to clear your head, then try again with a different image.

Auras and Aura Reading

Surely you have heard of the aura, its colors, and reading. I will tell you about it and how to learn to read it.

What Are Auras?

Simply put, the aura is a light energy or electromagnetic field that surrounds all beings in an ellipse and cannot be detected with the naked eye. The aura is the union of the etheric, emotional, and physical bodies and is a message for our soul. Auras are associated with chakras.

Aura Reading

The aura generally extends from one to three feet in all directions of the body, surrounding the person like a multi-layered "egg of light." The aura is said to consist of seven layers or subtle bodies (some say 12 or more) that are constantly interrelated and influencing each other.

1. **The etheric body:** This is the closest to the physical body, and it generally reflects our physical health and our most basic instincts. It usually appears as a soft blue or silver color, but with the disease, it can darken, especially around the affected areas.
2. **The emotional body:** As its name suggests, it reflects a person's state of mind and emotional responses to other people and situations. As such, it is the most unstable layer of the aura, constantly changing

with one's emotions. However, the residues of the strongest emotions, such as anger and fear, are stored in this layer for some time, affecting a person's emotional and physical health over time. Each emotion produces a different color in the emotional layer of the aura, so it can manifest in any shade or combination of colors. The brightest and purest colors usually indicate elevated emotions and peace. Cloudy colors are more representative of strong emotions or instincts.

3. **The mental layer or body:** This is related to what we call consciousness. The conscious thoughts and intentions of the individual are reflected in this layer. Yellow and orange are the characteristic colors of the spiritual body. People with a high IQ are said to have bright yellow mental bodies.

4. **The astral body:** This is connected to the physical body by the silver cord and reflects our higher aspirations and spiritual advancement in unconditional love. It is something like a portal to other dimensions, and it is said that it can be disembodied and transported freely in what is called astral projection. It's also partly about our willpower. It can appear in various colors, from pure pink to a mix of all rainbow colors.

5. **The spirit body:** This is really about connection and communication with others, with ourselves, and with our higher purpose.

6. **The higher or celestial body:** This is the connection between our human consciousness and the spiritual plane where dreams and memories of other beings or out-of-body experiences are often found.

7. **The divine body:** This is the connection to the higher planes and divine wisdom and can manifest as lightning and brilliant golden light. The more the individual becomes separated from their higher purpose and spiritual path, the more attenuated or blocked this aura becomes.

How Are Auras Read?

In order to see the bright colors of your aura or someone else's, you need a neutral background. Find a white or neutral wall or background. If you want to see your aura, you also need a mirror. If you don't have a mirror, you can place it on a white surface or a piece of paper to read the aura around your hand. Make sure you are in a comfortable and quiet environment so that you can focus without interruptions.

Relax your eyes while looking at it. Pick a spot to look at and watch for 30 to 60 seconds. Make your eyes slightly out of focus while focusing on the peripheral vision area. You may start to see fog around the edges. It may appear clear or white. After a while, it can become the color of the aura. Focus on a small area at first. On the subject, it may help to see the halo around the head if the forehead is the focal point. If you want to read your own aura, you can focus on the area around your head or look at your fingertips on a piece of white paper. In this case, use your nails as the focal point.

If you start to see colors, they may be bright or cloudy. Some people, especially beginners, can only see one dominant color, while others can see multiple colors. The more you practice reading your aura, the more colors and variations you can see. It just takes time and practice.

Learn About Red Auras

According to aura readers, people with a red aura tend to be energetic, enthusiastic, adventurous, and quick-tempered. They can be strong, competitive, and athletic. They are usually direct, straightforward, and honest, but they often need to be first.

Analyzing the Blue Aura

Aura interpreters describe people with blue auras as excellent communicators with insight, eloquence, charm, and intelligence.

Learn About Yellow Auras

As described by aura connoisseurs, people with a yellow aura appear intelligent, analytical, creative, logical, critical of themselves and others, eccentric, and pushy, but can be a workaholic. They often choose their friends carefully and are not easily lonely. In some cases, they may be more prone to depression and become withdrawn. They can confidently handle themselves in front of a crowd. Organized and inspiring. They may be trying to balance their minds and hearts to make difficult decisions. They tend to help calm the anger of others and are mediators.

Meet the Orange Aura

People with an orange aura are often described as generous, social, honest, kind, affectionate, empathetic, sensitive, and charming. They can also be impatient and end relationships quickly. They can be a bit moody, but they are also quick to forgive and forget.

Interpretation of the Pink Aura

Aura readers describe these people as generous, loving, affectionate, loyal, wholesome, and romantic. Once they find a mate, they usually remain faithful. They usually welcome family and friends into the home and can be gracious hosts. They seem to have high morals and can't stand injustice in the world.

Interpretation of the Purple Aura

Those said to have a purple aura can be sensitive, mystical, philosophical, intuitive, knowledgeable, admirable, and in harmony with animals and nature. They can be selective with their friends and maintain close relationships with them. They are often unlucky in love, but once they find a partner, they are often very committed.

Analyze the Golden Aura

If someone has a golden aura, they are likely rakish, persistent, generous, sociable, proud, and independent. They tend to surround themselves with beauty and can't bear to expose their flaws. They also like to entertain and earn the attention and admiration of others.

Black Aura

A black aura is associated with hatred, depression, and serious illness. People with a black aura can be considered miserable and ordinary.

Four Types of Psychic Intuition

These are the four types of intuition:

Clairaudience

Clairaudient's message sounds like someone is speaking in your head. The sound is never harsh or haunting (unlike what someone with certain psychological conditions, severe hormonal imbalances, or vitamin and mineral deficiencies might hear). The tone of this voice is almost always the same: quiet and calm.

Clairvoyance

Some people use the word "clairvoyance" as a synonym for "psychic," but clairvoyance is actually just one of four types of psychic power that psychics use. Clairvoyant information comes to mind in the form of an image or scene and is often in the form of a metaphor. If the customer is overwhelmed, you may see them choking or carrying a large bag. If you see images of continental plates shifting or an earthquake shaking under someone's feet, it means the client is going through such dramatic life changes that nothing is stable.

Clairsentience

The message of clairsentience arrives as a feeling, and clairsentience is the most common of the four types of psychic power. Intuition, being able to read the emotions of others, or feeling the collective energy of a room all fall under this umbrella. Before I speak to a client on the phone, I can usually get an idea of their energy: lively, serious, outgoing, highly intelligent, nurturing... I get chills every time I send a message to a customer, and I know it's important that the customer listen.

If someone has physical discomfort, I usually feel it briefly in my own body before or during the call. (My knees hurt if the client just had surgery there, or my stomach hurts if they have a digestive problem.) If a client's throat chakra (the way we express ourselves and our emotions) is closed, my throat often feels tight briefly during sessions.

Claircognizance

How do I know if my client's parents are narcissistic or if my client's child is highly difficult? How do I overcome subconscious barriers and old wounds that are holding my client back, or how do I instantly understand my client's complex relationships with friends and colleagues? This intuitive ability is called claircognizance. This occurs when our intuition is instantly downloaded into our brains, just like when you download large amounts of information onto your computer's hard drive. Although when it happens in a human brain, the download happens in just a few seconds. Don't wait for large files to load—your intuition helps!

Chapter 2
How to Improve Psychic Abilities

Guided by the objective of this book, I want you to know how to improve your psychic abilities so that you can understand and take care of yourself. For this reason, I will talk to you about self-love, strengthening your psychic abilities, vibrations, and general and own energy.

Increase Self-Esteem

Low self-esteem is behind most mental and emotional problems and is an obstacle to happiness and connecting with the beautiful energies of life. If you are wondering how to improve your self-esteem, you are in the right place. Low self-esteem can cause difficulties in your social relationships; you are afraid to get close to the people you like or you sabotage yourself in the pursuit of your life goals. Self-esteem is the way we express our feelings about our actions, attitudes, abilities, achievements, and failures. It is our sense of worth and our appreciation of ourselves. It is a relationship that we have built with "ourselves" over the years, and it is based on how we respond to situations that arise in our lives.

Strengthen Psychic Abilities

Some psychics are stronger in one psychic realm or choose to specialize in one at the expense of others. Imagine that you are using your "third eye," the chakra (or energy field) that sits above your actual eyes. Imagine opening and dilating this third eye. See what you notice on the "internal screen" of your mind. Try this with your eyes closed.

Clairvoyance means that you can see mental images. One aspect of clairvoyance is "remote viewing," which is the ability to see things not known to common sense. It works through the aura to receive impressions from the communicating spirit. For remote viewing, determine the remote location to detect. Close your eyes and think about the location. Shift your intention upward toward your third eye and write down your first impressions.

Clairaudience is the ability to receive mental impressions in the form of sound. The words are transmitted through the aura to the medium's subconscious mind as if the medium were a telephone. To practice clairaudience, repeat a word in your head while you think about it. This helps develop your inner voice.

Practice your psychic abilities with small objects. Some psychics, such as those who work in criminal investigations, wear clothes. The key is to find an item that has been used, as the psychic believes that it has more power than an unused item. Put the object in your hand, close your eyes, relax, and feel the sensations of your body. You may be wondering if you think the item belonged to a man or a woman, what the mood of the person who owned it is, and what kind of work they did.

Write down your instincts. This is called an energy footprint. Don't edit anything. It's better if the person who gave you the item actually knew the owner and didn't tell you. In this way, you can compare what you wrote with the real situation. Meditate to develop your psychic abilities. This will clear your mind and better focus on your sixth sense. Reducing confusion is very important.

Learn to trust and recognize intuition. Intuition is a belief or feeling that is not based on logical reasoning. It is a perception that transcends logic. Although everyone has intuition, some people can develop it better than others. Cultivate your intuition by trusting it. It is what you feel when you meet someone for the first time. Make sure your motives are pure, as this will release psychic tendencies.

Be aware of random thoughts and feelings. Keep a journal handy at all times, and try to write down thoughts that seem to come out of nowhere. After a while, you may notice that patterns tend to emerge. Thoughts that previously seemed completely random and unrelated begin to form recognizable themes or ideas.

Allowing yourself a few minutes of silence upon waking will make it easier to remember your dreams in more detail than getting up in the morning and rushing to start your day. Try setting your alarm to wake up 10 to 15 minutes before your normal wake-up time. Give yourself some time to remember your dream and make some quick notes in your journal. The subconscious is most rampant during sleep.

The Energetic Vibration of Life

The second universal law, the law of vibration, assumes that everything (every atom, object, and living being) is in constant motion, vibrating at a specific frequency. The speed at which something vibrates is called its frequency, and the only difference between one object and another is its frequency of vibration. You can think of this frequency as vibratory energy. Someone's energy, or the energy of a physical space or a group of people, is not something you can see or touch but something you can feel.

The idea behind this law is not only that we all have a specific vibrational frequency but that we can also learn to tune our vibrations if we get caught up in lower vibrational experiences or scenarios. The more you tune into your energy, the more you can see how its vibration affects your entire experience. Considering that the reality of our external physical world is in a constant state of vibration, we must know that this vibratory energy moves in the form of waves, having a range of amplitudes and frequencies that give it different characteristics and behaviors.

In the case of sound, it is no longer a series of waves created by a vibrating object that, when detected, causes the receptor (such as the eardrum) to vibrate. Any sound is made up of waves of different frequencies. To make this concept easier for you, take a look at this nice experiment in which a series of sounds of different frequencies are played on a surface with grains of salt. With each sound, different geometric patterns are created with such precision that they are more reminiscent of magic than science.

Why Do People Pray

All prayers, regardless of religion, have some power, but some techniques are more powerful than others. For centuries, what some have described as miraculous healing has occurred through the proper use of prayer.

Now, what is prayer? Prayer is a way of transferring energy from point A (the person who prays) to point B (the person who needs the prayer). The energy of prayer is carried safely to its destination by the power of love. The ancient yogis referred to the spiritual energy transmitted from the supplicant [i.e., the prayer] to the recipient as "*prana*" or "universal life force." But the carrier of this energy is love.

Keep Positivity

A positive mindset makes all the difference when it comes to enjoying the opportunities that life offers us. It's just that some people unknowingly focus on the bad all the time, not realizing that the time they spend lamenting is something they do to sabotage themselves.

Part of happiness has to do with objective and material basic needs, while other parts have to do with mindset, attention management, and frequency of positive thinking. We need to learn new habits of positive attitude all the time so that we can achieve the goals we set for ourselves. A positive attitude improves your self-esteem and your behavior so that you can be successful in everything you set out to do.

Positive thinking is looking for the best in the worst. There is always something good to be found in everything, and expect the best for you even when things around you look bad. Best of all, when you're looking for good things, you can always find them. This is something worth investigating. Having a positive attitude can make us see the world in a better light, even when the problem is not as bad as it seems.

These are some tips that will help you have a good attitude:

1. Increase your self-esteem.
2. Focus on everything you can control.
3. Distance yourself from negative opinions.
4. Identify the good things you have in your life.
5. Direct your thoughts to specific objectives.
6. Surround yourself with people with a positive attitude.

In short, to have a more positive attitude, it is important not to hold back, not to let ourselves be trapped by hopelessness, and make us see things with a negative bias. To do this, we must work with clear and realistic objectives in our day to day and choose social environments that lead us to bring out the best in ourselves.

Manifest Favorable Conditions

Bringing positive energy is possible. These tips will help you on the way to having favorable conditions in your life.

Everything Is Possible

One of the things that takes the most energy from you is struggling with who you are and where you are. It's hard to accept that you're not where you want to be or that you're not reaching your goals, especially if you've already worked hard to achieve them. The reality is that we all complain about what we have from time to time. But will it really make a positive difference? To attract positive energy, learn to accept and take responsibility for your unhappiness.

To Attract Positive Energy: Laugh

Laughter is an important behavior to becoming a more positive person. You must learn to laugh at the negative situations that happen to you and yourself. When you do this, you will have more tolerable relationships. When these moments arise, learn to share them with others. The only thing you should avoid is making fun of others to feel superior or make others feel bad.

Find Out What You Want and Need

The next step to attract positive energy is really complicated because we are changing sentient beings. Also, the vast majority of people have a hard time understanding what is expected of them in life, let alone what they need. However, what you can do is pay attention to the things that you don't want or that make you unhappy. They will give you a more precise clue as to what your values are and where you should focus your energy.

To Attract Positive Energy: Let Go of Your Past

Negative energy is formed in the past, while positive energy exists in the present and the future. Many of us have experienced tragedies that keep us from moving on, but if you accept them and allow yourself to live for today, you will have a better tomorrow.

Attracting positivity is not about forgetting or burying the past but about accepting it and being grateful for the lessons taught. Then move on with more knowledge and maturity.

Change Your Focus

If you really want to attract positivity, it's important to pay attention to the way you see things. Now, it is not about denying the negative and blinding yourself only to see the good. If you do this, you will end up creating more problems in your life. What you have to do is learn to put things in perspective and recognize the good, even in the opposite situation. Have you ever been fired because something went wrong at work? Well, do not think that you are not lucky professionally; remember that now you have the potential to look for something better.

How to Channel More Positive Energy into Your Life

Learn the concepts of how to channel energy and attract the best into your life.

Meditate and Seek Calm

Finding inner and outer peace fills your mind with bliss. Inner peace helps you accept who you are, and your inner dialogue fills you with joy. External peace improves your relationships with those around you. That does not mean that you become an extremist of meditation and Buddhism. It's just about understanding that everything you do has consequences in your life. If you are a good person, you always behave well and bring something positive to your life; that is what you attract.

Let the Emotions Flow

When you feel emotions, learn to express them. Not everything is perfect, and it is normal to have some bad energy inside of you, such as sadness or anger. It is important to learn to expel them. Once you have pushed the negativity out of your body, there is room to attract the positive.

Here is a variety of options until you find the one that best suits your needs, but try to stay positive:

1. Hit a cushion.
2. Shout.
3. Do intense exercise.
4. Cry.
5. Go running.

Think of emotions as pure energy. Use it for something positive, like improving your health or achieving a new goal. If you are someone who holds on to all the emotions you have experienced, over time, they can become a burden.

Surprise Yourself Periodically

From time to time, weekly or monthly, dedicate part of your income and time to different activities such as:

1. Go to the beach.
2. Go to the zoo.
3. Climb a mountain.
4. See a friend you haven't contacted in a while.

What matters is that you don't have a plan but that you can enjoy the unexpected. You will find that this helps you attract positive energy without exerting yourself. Getting outside for outdoor activities should be at the top of your list. These can relax you and fill your lungs with fresh air. You will see that, in a short time, you forget about the negative.

Chapter 3

Understanding Empaths and Knowing Their Powers

I n this chapter, you will have a vision of the powers of empathy and the best superpowers that you can develop with psychic empathy.

How to Use Your Own Superpowers to Have an Impact on the World

For many people, the first step in harnessing their extrasensory abilities is to separate the concept from the deception. While there are certainly plenty of charlatans who exaggerate their abilities or make them up entirely for business, these people are not psychics—they are con artists who use scare tactics to pray to unsuspecting or vulnerable people. In many cases, pretending to be a psychic is just one of many types of exploitation out there.

On the other hand, a psychic is simply someone who can see, hear, feel, taste, or have an intuition that goes beyond the physical plane. It's difficult, if not impossible, for you to definitively define what society takes to be "normal." After all, we are conditioned to believe that our perception of reality is very punctual—it is assumed that everyone is certain that the sky is blue or that we can tell that someone is in a bad mood. But as we continue to expand this sensory spectrum, we soon realize that certain senses are becoming less common by the day among our peers. Through this awareness, many of us become aware of our unique and innate psychic gifts.

For the most part, mental abilities develop during childhood. These gifts help people who directly or indirectly teach a language or are cultivated according to environmental conditions. When we're little, we notice more, see more, hear more, and feel more—these are basic survival instincts that help us move safely through the world. But as we mature, we are told not to be so sensitive; ghosts are not real, pain is always physical... Through this conditioning, we come to believe that emotion and intuition are the antitheses of science and reason. We suppress our gifts, laugh at "clairvoyance," and accept the physical realm as all that reality.

The True Potential and Responsibilities of Psychic Empaths

While many people believe that everyone has some degree of psychic ability, this ability can come in many different forms. For some, psychic ability manifests as the ability to become what is known as empathy. Empathy is the ability to feel the feelings and emotions of others without them verbally telling us what they think and feel. Often psychics need to learn basic protection techniques. Otherwise, they may feel exhausted after absorbing the energy of others.

The psychological form of empathy should not be confused with the basic human emotion of empathy. Most people can empathize with another human being, but not necessarily with a psychic. The main difference, however, is that a person with psychic abilities usually detects from non-visual and non-verbal cues that another person is feeling pain, fear, or pleasure. Sometimes it's about detecting energy fields or auras; other times, you can just "know" that the person is feeling a certain way, even though there are no obvious clues.

In many cases, empaths are trained to detect subtle changes in the energetic vibrations of others. Most empaths are good listeners and tend to pursue careers that use this ability to help others: for example, social work, counseling, energy work like reiki, and ministry. Others are often drawn to empaths because they feel comfortable talking to them. In fact, you may notice that empaths are overly polite and usually don't want to hurt anyone's feelings, so they often let people talk to them, even if they'd rather be somewhere else.

Jola is an empath who lives in Minnesota and works as a nurse at a physical therapy rehab center. She says, "When I first entered nursing, I was working in pediatric oncology. I could not stand it. I was so sensitive to aches and pains that I would cry all the way home after every shift. Now, I continue to work with people who needed my help, but I wasn't emotionally ready to work in oncology because I was so sensitive." She added that working on grounding, shielding, and centering has helped her a lot.

While we don't yet understand how empathy works, we do have some information. Everything has a vibration or vibrating frequency, and empathy can feel these vibrations and even identify invisible things to the naked eye. The slightest change or all five senses.

If you consider yourself a psychic, you should definitely learn protective techniques to help protect your emotions. Furthermore, it is also important to realize that being emotionally sensitive does not automatically make you empathic. Many people without empathy still pay attention to other people's feelings and emotions because it's human nature. If you really can't relate to others due to emotional turmoil, it may be a good idea to seek the services of a mental health professional; likely, what you are experiencing is not metaphysical in nature at all.

If you think you are an empathetic person and you can't handle it, try giving yourself the privilege of being alone. A lot of empathy is very introverted, and being around people can be mentally and emotionally draining if you don't protect yourself effectively. If you feel exhausted, take some alone time and recharge your batteries. In particular, give yourself the option to reconnect with nature; you may find this more beneficial than sitting indoors alone. Remember that empathy is just one of many metaphysical abilities. Clairvoyance is the ability to see hidden things. It is sometimes used for remote viewing and is sometimes believed to help people find missing children and locate lost items.

You may have heard the term "medium" when talking about psychic abilities, especially those that involve communication with the spirit world. Traditionally, a medium is someone who speaks to the dead in some way. In the end, intuition is the ability to simply "know" things without being told. Many empaths are excellent tarot card readers, as this skill gives them an advantage when reading cards for clients. This is sometimes called clairvoyance.

The Difficulties of Being an Empath

Because empaths are constantly bombarded with the energy around them, they often become overstimulated. Even in seemingly peaceful circumstances, if one person's negativity enters your bubble, it can tear you apart.

You Can Fight the Limitations

Empaths may have trouble setting boundaries. On one hand, they want to help others, but they also do not always know how to "turn off" their own abilities. This makes it very important that empaths learn to stay out of the heads of their observers or witnesses, so they don't always absorb everything.

You Can Feel the Emotions of Other People

One of the most fundamental aspects of empathy is feeling the emotions of others. Empathic people can easily pick up on your discomfort, even when you haven't said anything, because they suddenly start to feel it in their own bodies.

You Are Overwhelmed by the Crowd

For an empath who hasn't mastered the protective psychological bubble, being in a crowd is not a fun place to be. You absorb not only the energy of those around you but also the energy of the whole group and the general energy of the physical space. It's too much!

You Have to Actively Choose Not to Let the Energy In

Do you find it difficult to block the energy of others? It's a show of empathy, Richardson noted, adding that it's important for these people to learn to consciously separate themselves from others, a "skill that needs to be acquired and honed."

The Inability to Say "No"

Empaths want to help ease someone else's pain because they can feel it in their own bodies. This makes them natural helpers or healers. Others often recognize this quality in themselves and turn to empaths for help. Because you connect with people, you naturally become loving and compassionate.

Empaths draw their energy not only from the person but also from the physical space. Empaths can be greatly influenced by a particular space and how it is maintained. This can be a good thing or a bad thing; a positive vibe can be very uplifting, and a negative vibe can be especially stifling. The fact that you can't say "no," makes you always be exposed to this, which leads you to feel exhausted and overwhelmed.

Television Becomes a Challenge

Especially when you discover yourself, you find out that the media overwhelms you and misrepresents the beautiful gift that you possess. This is challenging because you are filled with many wrong theories. Many empaths have always been empaths, often first displaying their acute sensitivity as children and then expanding on it over time. However, empaths may also open their eyes to their gifts later in life. This is because when the empath is young and does not discover their sensitivity, they can unconsciously close it to preserve their energy.

Susceptibility to Addictions

Addictions are prone to everything that comes hand in hand with what has been said in this subchapter since, on some occasions, you may not know how to handle psychic empathy and have many feelings that, if you do not channel them correctly, in the end, you could end up in different types of addictions such as drug addiction, alcoholism, or any action of low vibration that affects you. In order to channel it, you have to work on your emotional intelligence your self-love, and on your way to growing by accepting everything you have and what you lack.

See Through Others

Seeing through others is good on many occasions, but it can also be very exhausting. Constant fatigue comes from a permanent state of being over-stimulated and overwhelmed by your surroundings. We all have a certain radius of perception. I mean, some of us only feel things when we're really close to people. Others clearly feel things from all over the world. Some people can feel not only through space but also through time. They can hold an object and connect with people who have touched the object in the past. Therefore, to detach from their feelings, the empath needs to be alone in a very secluded place.

Privacy Management

Many empaths tend only to have a few close friends. They avoid superficial gatherings and crowds. However, sometimes when they want to spend time with friends, they need more alone time. If you never spend time with your friends, they usually don't stick around. Often as an empath, you learn things that your friends don't. If you push too hard or say things they aren't ready to hear, you will destroy the friendship.

You can't choose when to empathize and when not to. Other people's thoughts and emotions intrude on your life all the time, even when you sleep. You can stop it, but it takes constant effort and can be exhausting. Without realizing it, you learn things about random people that you never wanted to know. Intimacy is altered, as you can see when you work on empathy and have this gift.

Socialization Problems

A friend who is an empath colleague told me one day: "I sat in a coffee shop and reviewed the results of my final exam online. I still vividly remember my world crashing down as I stared at the little numbers on the computer screen, telling me that I had failed, had to retake the exam, and was at risk of being thrown out of Oxford if I didn't do well enough next time. My face is straight, but my heart is broken. A woman my mother's age sat across from me. She impulsively handed me a cup of tea that she had just bought (she is British) and said to me, 'I don't know what you're going through, but I know you'll get over it,' as she put down her tea. She silently grabbed my shoulders and left without saying anything else."

Super empaths can recognize when those around them are hurting, no matter how strong they appear to the outside world. Of course, this is a benefit in terms of helping those around you, but sometimes it can be hard to know when to stop for your own good. No matter how badly they behave, no one believes that they are bad people. If you have super empathy, it means that you also believe that no one is a bad person. It is too easy for you to understand another person's point of view. A friend of mine was caught cheating. Her boyfriend was so empathetic that he actually told me that he could have been a better boyfriend to keep her from feeling like a 1950s housewife. Because she believes that her actions are justified, he does too.

If you find that you really can't call someone a bad person or point out the negative qualities of a toxic friend, take a moment to practice empathy with yourself. What will make you happy? How do you feel? It's better to do it yourself than to talk to a friend; otherwise, you could be telling them what you think they want to hear instead of what's going on inside you.

Socializing has several points that affect you:

* You always see the good in people, which can prevent you from seeing bad things.
* They want to know more or question you.
* They take you for being crazy or a charlatan.

Socializing represents one more challenge when you have this gift.

Fatigue

If you find yourself exhausted from dealing with friends, family, or even strangers, it's time to set limits. For example, make it a rule not to answer late-night calls or texts, or direct people to relevant resources, like a therapist or hotline, rather than trying to solve the world's problems on your own.

Depression and Anxiety

Like any superpower, empathy has positive and negative aspects. But as more and more empathy workshops are taught, since we want to know everyone's secret thoughts or feelings, its downsides are also worth remembering. Super empaths often have no idea who they are when they are alone. They try to carry the load of everyone around them. They have difficulty being objective with others and often know too much to make those around them feel comfortable.

If you notice any of these negative traits, you may be more of an empath than you think. As long as you maintain your boundaries, prioritize alone time, and take time to reflect deeply on those around you, you can ensure your superpower doesn't overwhelm you, and you can use it forever.

Your Capacity for Love and Compassion Is Magnified

As an empath, your ability to feel love and empathy for others is on a different level. One of the most difficult obstacles in a relationship is usually mutual understanding. Sure, we can try to explain our feelings to the other person, but they don't really understand how we feel. It takes a lot of time and effort to really put yourself in someone else's shoes. As an empath, that door is open, and you can't help but feel the full power of your partner's inner feelings.

This allows you to develop a level of love and compassion that is difficult for others to achieve. This can help you improve your relationships and better empathize with others, even those with whom you disagree. You understand the feelings of others and can find common ground, instantly developing great compassion and motivating you to act more kindly and peacefully.

Chapter 4
Benefits of Being an Empath

In the previous chapters, you have been able to learn about the personalities of empathic people. I also told you about the disadvantages and how being an empath affects you. Now, I dedicate this chapter to the advantages.

Empaths are great problem solvers because they can see beyond what others see. Not to mention that many have the gift of being leaders or key players in teams, their personalities tend to be creative and magnetic, and they can get wherever they want. Also, when they want to, they can have very lucid and vivid dreams, as if they were real. They can create strong and unbreakable bonds with others, with total synchronicity and frequent *déjà vu*. Let's see some other advantages of being an empath:

It Is Difficult for People to Manipulate Them

They are so aligned with the way people act, talk, move, and feel that they pay close attention to true intentions. They can easily spot even the subtlest hints of deception. This means that they are more likely to know when someone is lying or manipulating them based solely on how it makes them feel. Their empathy has built-in crap radar, which is a huge plus.

They Can Read a Room

Since they are attentive not only to their own emotions but also to those of everyone around them, they can feel the vibrations in the room almost instantly. More often than not, they defuse situations and become peace-makers because they can know exactly where to go and avoid emotional land mines.

Likewise, they can almost always tell how someone feels about them by seeing how they react to what they say or do. Have you ever felt that someone had no vibration in your conversation? Where do you know you should slow down and move on? Many people cannot read the emotions and reactions of others effectively. These are great tips for making friends, dating, and landing job interviews.

They Know How Someone Affects Our Energy

Knowing how someone makes us feel has advantages for many reasons. Those who make you feel happy, warm, motivated, and loved are the ones to surround yourself with and hold on to. Anyone who makes you feel beaten up, sad, inferior, or angry is someone you should separate from or at least spend as little time with as possible. We need to protect our energy, and as empaths, we can detect energy spirits and energy vampires.

They Are Naturally Creative

Empaths possess the power to see the world very vividly, often in a different way than other people. They are also intuitive and long to be set free through creativity. Whether through music, writing, painting, or acting, we all need to build and create.

They Like to Help People

When you absorb the energy around you, you want the world to be happier and brighter. They are also more likely to offer the time and words of wisdom to those who they feel or think are sad or struggling because they can feel their emotions on another level. They also become more aware of how family, friends, and colleagues are feeling at any given time, of course. Often, they pull someone aside, ask if they're okay, and offer the support they may not know they need.

They May Feel Your Pain, but They Also Feel Your Love

Have you ever caught yourself crying during a happy scene in a movie? Or watching videos of adopted puppies, returning soldiers, and future grandparents tearing up your cheeks? Yes, we can feel other people's pain, and it can be exhausting and frustrating. But we are also lucky to feel their moments of love and happiness as if they were our own.

Empathy makes it easy to notice and adapt to the emotions of others. You see pain and suffering in everyone around you. You may also find it easy to absorb the feelings of others. You are very in tune with your environment and everyone in it. Empaths are very aware of subtle changes and are easily overstimulated by sounds, smells, noises, and crowds. While empathy can be difficult at times, there are many benefits to empathy.

They Have Great Creativity

Empathy is very creative. Since you draw so much from your environment, the creative outlet provides a means of expression. You put a lot of emotion and energy into everything you create. As a result, your creative efforts often impress others. Therefore, you can be quite successful in any field that requires creativity. This includes working as a writer, artist, dancer, actor, or chef. If you don't work in a creative field, you will benefit from a hobby that allows you to be creative.

Good Intuition

As an empath, you are very intuitive. When you absorb the emotions of others, you trust your intuition to make sense of it all. This allows you to notice subtle changes in body language, facial expressions, and tone of voice. Easily spot differences in the communicated content. Because of this, you will be able to tell when other people are being dishonest.

Useful

It is normal for empaths to want to help others. This is not limited to friends and family. You may also go out of your way to help others. Because you are so good at understanding what others are experiencing, you often know what kind of help will be most effective. Your trusting nature and kindness draw others to you, especially those in need. People are looking for valuable advice and great listening skills. Helping others makes you feel good because it fills you with positive emotions, enhancing your ability to help.

Compassionate

Empaths have a lot of compassion and understanding. It is easy for you to show kindness to others and stand up for the underdog. You really enjoy being around natural things, small children, and animals. Naturally, they are also attracted to you. Seeing others in trouble can cause great discomfort. Your compassion has no limits. You have a strong desire to comfort anyone who is suffering emotionally, physically, or mentally.

Awareness

Because you are so attuned and empathetic to your environment, you are very aware of any changes that occur. This can help you avoid embarrassing or even dangerous situations. The energy of a place is immediately noticeable and deeply felt. When the atmosphere in the room is positive, it lifts your spirits and makes you feel good. Similarly, you are aware when something is wrong with someone close to you. Because you know full well that you can provide a safe space for others to share, and you usually know exactly what they need.

Healing Energy

Empathy has a very healing energy. Others tend to calm down just by being in your presence. Feeling another person's pain makes you more aware of what they need most. When you learn about another person's pain, you also learn about what can help you. Empaths tend to listen carefully, and the ability to understand someone can help you.

Feel the Emotions of Others

As an empath, you not only notice other people's emotions, you feel them as well. This allows you to gain a deeper understanding of others. If you are with an emotional person, you too can experience the emotion. When you are with someone positive and happy, you experience these wonderful feelings just as intensely as if they were your own. This will make you feel great.

Experience Feelings Deeply

In addition to intensely experiencing other people's feelings as an empath, emotions are also felt deeply. If you feel some emotions more intensely, like sadness or fear, you can process them faster because you allow yourself to feel them so deeply. When you feel more positive emotions, you also feel them fully. This allows you to relive the pleasurable experience of creating a good feeling, allowing you to feel that feeling again.

Meaningful Relationships

Empath does not like superficial relationships. Therefore, empaths often have very deep and meaningful relationships. This is true for both friendships and romantic relationships. Since empaths are naturally understanding and compassionate, they are more likely to forgive others. This helps improve the quality and duration of relationships. You are always there to offer support when someone close to you is hurting.

Enjoy Time Alone

Alone time is key to empathy. You need time to process your feelings and separate your emotions from those of others. Alone time gives you a chance to relax and daydream. Since you trust your instincts so much and have a rich imagination, alone time can help you strengthen both. When you're alone, you can recharge your battery, so you don't feel overwhelmed by overstimulation. While being an empath can be challenging, there are many benefits as well. If you're struggling with some of the challenges of being an empath, one-on-one counseling can help. By focusing on the benefits of being an empath, you can improve your overall emotional health.

Chapter 5

How to Heal and Protect Your Energy—Taking Care of Yourself

Your energy is wonderful and you have to take care of it. In this chapter, I will teach you a series of tools that you can introduce into your life, such as guided meditations, breathing to channel, techniques to shield yourself, visualizations, and energy limitations, among many other elements that will help you take care of yourself.

Guided Meditation Experiences

People may want to open their third eye or sixth chakra for various reasons. Some believe that the third eye, also known as the brow chakra, is the gateway to higher consciousness and spiritual development. Others believe that it can help improve intuition, spiritual awareness, and psychic abilities. Others believe that it can help improve mental clarity and focus. Here is a brief overview of some ideas to help you get started:

1. Begin by doing some meditative exercises. Meditation will help you clear your mind and focus on your inner cognitions, thoughts, and feelings.
2. Practice some yoga poses. Yoga is a great way to open the seven chakras and energy centers.
3. Visualize a light on the forehead, between the eyebrows, and in the

third eye chakra. Focus on your inner thoughts and feelings while visualizing this light.
4.   Discover breathing techniques to help activate your third eye.
5.   Drink plenty of water. The more hydrated you are, the better your energy flow will be.
6.   Eat healthy food. Foods rich in antioxidants and nutrients will help you maintain your energy levels and overall health.

Pineal and Pituitary Glands

The pineal and pituitary glands are located in the brain and are responsible for producing some of the hormones that regulate our sleep cycles and mood. Some glands are connected to the third eye chakra. The pineal gland is a small, pea-shaped gland in the brain located near the center of the brain, just behind the eyes. The pineal gland produces melatonin, a hormone that regulates the sleep-wake cycle. Melatonin production is higher at night and lower during the day. It is believed that when the glands are working as they should, they help keep our energy levels balanced and our minds clear.

Meditations for Empathy

There are many ways to meditate, but here is a simple one to get you started:

1.   Get into a comfortable position, keeping your spine straight. You can sit on a chair or on the floor.
2.   You are going to close your eyes and concentrate on your breathing. Inhale slowly and deeply through the nose. Hold your breath for a few seconds, then slowly exhale through your mouth.
3.   As you breathe, visualize a purple or white light in the center of your forehead. Breathe in the light and imagine it growing brighter and brighter. Keep breathing deeply and focus on the light.
4.   Imagine opening your third eye chakra. Imagine it expanding until

your entire field of vision is filled with light. Stare at it for as long as you want, then let it go.

Different Types of Meditation

Below are the types of meditation and their benefits:

Primordial Sound Meditation

Primary sound meditation is a mantra-based meditation technique rooted in the Vedic tradition of India. A mantra is a repeated phrase that helps us reach a state of relaxation and internalization that favors a meditative state. Mantras are not random words but sacred sounds used by the ancient sages in meditation due to their powerful harmonic effect.

Vipassana Meditation

Vipassana meditation allows you to see things as they are. It is also a traditional Buddhist meditation practice widely used in the West due to mindfulness. This type of meditation emphasizes awareness of the breath, regulating the air going in and out through the nose. It also focuses on marking the ideas and experiences that arise.

Zazen (Zen) Meditation

The translation of the Japanese word *zazen* means "to sit in meditation." Many people, when they imagine meditation, imagine a person on the floor with legs crossed, eyes closed, and fingers in a mudra position. This does not happen in *zazen* meditation. It is a way to achieve enlightenment.

Transcendental Meditation

Transcendental Meditation is another mantra-based meditation. Like primary sound meditation, whose origins date back to ancient India, each person is given a personal mantra of vibrational qualities to help calm the mind. Although the goals of the two forms of meditation are similar, there are many differences, including the mantra itself and how it is chosen, the meditation instructions, and the recommended meditation times.

Metta or Loving-Kindness Meditation

Metta, or loving-kindness meditation, has its meaning in unconditional kindness and friendship. This form of meditation also has its origin in Buddhist teachings, mainly Tibetan Buddhism. Scientific research has shown that compassion and this kind and loving form of meditation are especially helpful in enhancing empathy, positivity, acceptance, and compassion for oneself and others. Anyone with low self-esteem, high levels of self-criticism, and a desire to be more empathetic to others can benefit from this practice.

Kundalini Meditation

The main idea of this meditation is that thanks to this technique, the kundalini energy located at the base of the spine is awakened. When this energy is released, it travels up the spine, leading to an experience commonly known as Kundalini awakening, which ultimately leads to enlightenment. Kundalini meditation can include breathing techniques, mantras, mudras, and chants to harness the power of the subconscious mind. It is an energizing way to awaken the soul.

Chakra Meditation

The chakras are the energy centers of the body, and we have seven, each located in a different area of the body, each associated with a different energetic color, sound, and purpose. Chakra meditation can be very powerful, especially when focusing on one element of the physical or emotional body at a time. Many chakra meditations use sound, specific hand placement, and visualization techniques to connect with the chakras and their healing energies.

Tonglen Meditation

This type of meditation is from Tibetan Buddhism and is characterized by the fact that the practitioner connects with their own pain and works to overcome it. Our culture teaches us to avoid pain and run away from it, which is the exact opposite of what tonglen meditation does.

The Importance of Breathing (How to Breathe)

In addition to its important function, breathing is another way of delivering energy to our body. When we are stressed, due to constant tension and worry, we tend to use costal breathing, which is short and gasping. However, relearning to breathe can teach us to take in as much oxygen as possible, which is good for both the mind and body. The two most common ways to control our breathing to channel our tension and stress are through alternate breathing and abdominal breathing.

Abdominal Breathing

Lie on your back with your back straight, legs straight, feet apart and out, and hands on your ribcage (below your clavicle). The fingers of the hand should touch. Inhale while counting to five. Notice how the ribcage expands and how the fingers separate. Repeat the process of placing our hands on the lower ribcage and abdomen.

Guided Meditation Exercises for Psychic Empaths

Let us now understand the correct steps to perform the meditation below:

1. Choose a quiet place without noise.
2. Sit comfortably on the floor with your legs crossed and your back straight.
3. Close your eyes.
4. Relax your body and release tension.
5. Focus on each part of your body, release tension and take a deep breath.
6. Focus on your breathing. Feel how you feel more relaxed with each inhalation, and feel how your body releases all the accumulated stress as you exhale.
7. Now focus on the forehead between the eyes.
8. Imagine a golden reflection of a triangle entering your mind.
9. Then imagine that you can look inside your mind and see all your thoughts, experiences, and problems.
10. Feel how the bright light fills every corner of your soul.
11. Feel, in turn, how all your negative thoughts and experiences are leaving your mind through the window that you have opened for them.
12. Do not forget to breathe.
13. When you are satisfied, and your mind is clear, you can close the window.

Channel Your Energies with This Meditation

1. Find a comfortable place to sit and close your eyes.
2. Little by little, begin to connect with your breathing and your five senses since these two are the anchors that connect us with the present moment. I invite you to connect with this in an extended way here and now through them.

3. From here, I invite you to review your day and the situations that affected or interfered in some way with your sensory or emotional state. Many of these may be about other people and your interactions with them. Maybe receiving a message, the energy you feel from someone, the aggressiveness you feel after saying those words... Know the moments of your day that affect you.
4. While doing this, bring your attention to your body and be aware of where in your body you feel these accumulated charges and where are the residues of those situations.
5. Concentrate on those parts of your body and see how they feel without changing anything. Observe them as interesting things that happen to you.
6. Now, I invite you to imagine these feelings in some way. Maybe they have the faces of people you know, maybe they are just a splash of color. Visualize them your way and see them that way on those parts of your body.
7. As you look at them, notice the flow of your breath and also include it in your awareness.
8. Now I invite you to follow the natural flow of your breath and with each exhalation visualize these feelings arising in the form you have given them, gradually dissolving and disappearing in the rays of the sun in the sky. Observe this, simply by witnessing it.
9. As you release these charges, bring some of your attention to your body, being aware of the effect this has on it. Feel your body.
10. At your own pace, gently, you can open your eyes.

Shielding Techniques for Psychic Empaths

There are different ways in which you can protect yourself from bad energy and what this gift that you possess causes you:

Protection with Crystals

Crystals can absorb negative energy from your environment, making them the perfect shield for empathy. Simply placing one in the palm of your hand or placing one next to your bed while you sleep can do wonders to remove the negative energy you absorb throughout the day.

Black Tourmaline

Considered one of the best empathy crystals due to its powerful ability to absorb electromagnetic frequencies from the surrounding environment. Although there are many other crystals to clean energies that you can take advantage of.

Protection with Herbs and Plants

As with crystals, certain herbs and plants have protective properties that can help you balance your emotions. For centuries, tribes and cultures around the world have used them to reach a higher state of consciousness, allowing them to connect with divine power.

St. John's Wort

This herb has been used for centuries to ward off evil forces.

Protective Viewing

A screen protector is a very effective way to protect yourself from the outside world, but it can take some practice, so it may take you longer to master! Perform different visualization exercises, always seeing walls and everything you want to be a huge blockade that protects you.

White Light Protection

Do meditations where you see an immense white energy that surrounds and purifies you. You can use the meditation you want and when you reach relaxation in that part where you send white energy to your body or chakras, let it be an immense white light that surrounds you completely.

Meditation

Like the previous point, meditation will help you eliminate bad energy. Meditation is a way to focus on inner peace. It is an activity that allows you to be in the moment. When you recognize where you are and make peace with it, you can eliminate the negative energy that oppresses you and prevents you from improving. In other words, stop worrying about the past or the distant future. Enjoy life now because sooner than you think, it may be too late.

Energy Limits

This is a band of energy, a band of light that surrounds us and actually starts at the skin and penetrates the four to six-foot space around us, forming our second self. I mean, most of us are really familiar with our inside or have been trying to get familiar with that self. But sometimes it's hard to accept the fact that we are so much bigger than this body. We spread out in waves and bands of light and energies, literally four to six feet beyond us. We further extend these types of invisible but somewhat energetic bands of energy.

This Way, You Can Set the Energetic Limits

1. First, stop and actively disconnect from what you're doing. This can be done simply by taking a deep breath and saying the words that help you. I use the word "focus," and I have a friend who says, "I'm back." Anything that helps bring you to the present moment in your own body and detach yourself from whatever is going on.
2. Saying your name helps you come back to your own experience.

3. Ask yourself: "Is this my problem or my emotions?" If not, "Whose is it?"
4. Make an effort to say what happened. For example, "I just walked into a tense meeting."
5. Name five differences between you and other people. For example, I'm not wearing green; I'm a man; I'm with my son, etc. This will further help you separate yourself from others.

Define and Express Your Needs

More than telling other people, you have to tell yourself, you have to put yourself in a process where you can define and express the needs you have when you recognize those shortcomings and address them, whether they are emotional, peaceful, or overwhelmed by so many energies that you have had to work through.

Avoid Empathy Overload

I talked about this topic before; empathy can saturate you and make you feel bad, so when you feel like you can't take it anymore, you stop and clean yourself of overloads until you get better.

Exhale Negativity

One warning that you are absorbing someone's energy is to notice if you experience a sudden change in the physical or emotional state around that person. If you haven't felt anxious, depressed, tired, or down before, chances are the discomfort is at least partly theirs. If you walk away and the discomfort goes away, it's definitely not yours! However, sometimes a mood or symptom can be both yours and someone else's. You are more likely to carry unresolved emotional or physical pain. The more you deal with the issues that trigger you, the less likely you are to absorb other people's emotions.

When negativity hits you, immediately focus on breathing for a few minutes. Breathe in and out slowly and deeply to expel uncomfortable energy. Breathing circulates negativity out of your body. Holding your breath or breathing shallowly can trap negativity inside of you. As you breathe, I suggest you repeat this mantra three times out loud, firmly, in a tone that conveys your meaning: return to sender, return to sender, return to sender. The power of your voice can control the discomfort of your body. Your breath is the vehicle that transports it back to the universe.

Question Your Own Feelings

When you see your needs, you have to question your own feelings. Because on many occasions, you can feel bad, and when you evaluate your life, and you realize that everything seems to be "perfect," you do not understand why you are like this, but when you go deeper, it is because you have been absorbing other feelings, what has been contaminating you and you need to free yourself, which leads us to the next point

Step Back

When you're down, it's best to take a step back, whether you don't want to go somewhere because you feel bad energy, have a lousy job, or have a partner who doesn't make you feel good. Taking a step back is not a failure; it is survival to feel better about yourself.

Detox with Water

Bathing, showering, or washing your hands are good energy-cleansing rituals. The important part is to charge the water with your intention. An affirmation like "May this water cleanse my energy and make me feel fresh and clean" can help amplify your water-drinking ritual. You, too, can recharge your drinking water with the same intention and affirmation. When you drink it, it will help you clear your energy. Water is a living structuring element that connects directly with our energies and can be programmed to help us heal. Don't miss out on this powerful energy cleanse because it can be too easy. This is powerful!

Connect with Nature

Being in nature is one of the most effective ways in which you can effort-lessly clear your energy. Stand on the grass, sit under a tree, put your feet in the sea, sit by the river, any nature suits you. When you get out into nature intending to clear your energy, try basic exercises or just focus on taking deep breaths and visualizing your energy clearing.

Chapter 6

The Empath in the Workplace

Empathy at work is necessary. In this chapter, I will talk about the importance of living good human relationships and how to be an empathetic professional without fights or drama between colleagues.

Human Relations

Empaths and highly sensitive people tend to have a hard time working with others, despite being leaders. Noise and large groups, especially in the bustling industry when serving clients, can be overwhelming for empaths and can lead to anxiety and panic attacks. But there are many ways empaths can help build flow.

Are you an empathic or very sensitive person who finds it difficult to work with many people? It's overwhelming, right? For many of us, dealing with people is exhausting. It's not just stress in general. Working with people can be overwhelming for an empath, who absorbs subtle energies and is sensitive to them. We absorb all the energy and emotions around us like sponges, and the more people around us, the more information overload we have.

For example, when empathetic or highly sensitive people work in customer service, it feels like, well... have you ever taken a long trip in your car? You sit and listen to the radio all day, you nod to Taylor Swift, you arrive at your destination, you get out of the car, and you're like, "Oh my God, I'm defeated!" Mentally focus on the road. It is exhausting. For empaths, that's what being with a large group of people is all about. It is draining

Dynamics and Drama Among Colleagues

Successful empaths have a toolkit full of ideas, tips, tricks, insights, books, references, how-tos, guides, advice, and support groups for managing their energy, cultivating joy, and improving relationships, including working with people. You can do it. You can be a strong and compassionate person, outgoing and confident at work. All it takes is practice. Let us begin!

Successful Empath Meditates with Headphones

If you struggle with anxiety or feel overwhelmed when dealing with people, don't despair. It stands to reason that if you have a panic attack at work, the first thing you should do is calm down. There is nothing like learning to meditate. A strong meditation practice should be the cornerstone of any empath toolkit. Learning to sit still, quiet the mind, and relax can be beneficial in all areas of life, not just at work.

According to a ScienceDirect.com web article on the efficacy of meditation for anxiety disorders, "a previous study of 22 medical patients with DSM-III-R-defined anxiety disorders showed clinically and statistically significant improvements in subjective and objective symptoms of anxiety and panic following an 8-week outpatient physician-referred group stress reduction intervention based on mindfulness meditation."

You can use an app with your headphones on to relax, calm down, and be in the moment. You can learn to meditate by watching YouTube videos, taking classes, or reading books. Practicing this sense of calm and stillness will make it easier to evoke this state of being as you work. If you start to feel overwhelmed again at work, this mindfulness practice can help you immediately become aware of the adverse emotion so you can accept it, let it go, and return to a calm state.

The Successful Empath Prays

Well, let's talk about prayers. I believe there is a higher power out there. You shouldn't have a name for it per se, but when you pray, it is to this higher consciousness, this energy that connects everything. Pray to your spiritual self; your higher mind has all the answers. Seeking help and trusting in a source of wisdom and healing greater than your consciousness can imagine has proven to be of great benefit to those who need it.

A study titled *Prayer, Attachment to God, and Symptoms of Anxiety-Related Disorders among U.S. Adults,* conducted for the journal of the Association for the Sociology of Religion, found that your view of God must begin with secure attachment, but prayer will be beneficial. "In this context, prayer appears to confer emotional comfort, which results in fewer symptoms of anxiety-related disorders." said researcher Matt Bradshaw, Ph.D.

Before you start working, try saying a little prayer. Whatever help you need, fold your hands together or gently fold them in your lap and ask for guidance. Focus on the results and ideal scenarios that you want to achieve today. Say, "Universe, God, spirit world, higher self, I need help today. I am an empathetic person and am overwhelmed by the noise and energy at work. Please help me to be strong and confident so I can be productive at work. Help me stay positive and happy today. I could really use your help to protect my energy from all the crazy people I will see today. I promise I'll be back later; thank you!"

It is great if you are a religious person! But prayer is not a skill exclusive to advanced practitioners. Prayer can be the simple act of focusing the mind on an ideal reality and asking for help. Whether you believe in a higher power or not, praying and trusting that help is just around the corner is a powerful psychological tool for empaths in the workplace. Believing that you are not alone can take a load off your shoulders.

The Successful Empath Breathes

When it comes to the workplace, the number one way to introduce empathy is to breathe. Deep breathing exercises are the sandwich if your empathy toolkit is a lunch box. Guiding the management of empathy is essential. If you feel anxious, nervous, overwhelmed, or stressed at work, acknowledge this and congratulate yourself on realizing it. You usually find yourself subconsciously losing control. This is the first step, and paying attention to how you feel is half the battle.

The next step is to breathe, just breathe. Focus on your breathing. If you can, leave work and find a quiet place to reflect for five minutes—in your car, a bathroom stall, a stairwell, a short walk around the building, or anywhere you can get away from the hustle and bustle of the workplace. Next, take a deep breath and slowly count to four. Then slowly count to four and exhale. Repeat five or six times.

Running example: Inhale deeply and count to four slowly and intentionally: in, two, three, four. Exhale gently and let it go for a similar slow count of four: out, two, three, four. Similarly, in, two, three, four... and out, two, three, four. Repeat, in and out. Breathe slowly, in, two, three, four... and out, two, three, four. Breathe slowly and methodically. Relax and take a deep breath. Repeat this in-and-out cycle as many times as necessary.

Focus on your breath and notice where in your body you feel it. Do you feel your breath in your throat? Have you noticed your lungs expand and contract? Can you see how your belly expands with each breath? Do you feel the air go through your nostrils? Allow your breath to ease any anxiety or stress so that you can let it go. Relax and breathe. How do you feel now?

This simple yet powerful technique can be used almost anywhere, and once you master it, you'll be able to multitask and practice deep breathing while you work. I held my breath as I waited on customers at the register. I smile because I take pride in being able to take care of myself.

Empathic Professions

These are the professions that an empath can practice:

Registered Nurse

Nurses provide patient care, working in many settings, hospitals, schools, doctors' offices, surgery centers, or patients' homes. Depending on the type of care the patient requires and/or the area of medicine in which you are an expert (for example, pediatrics or emergency care), they may have responsibility for a variety of tasks in relation to the patient, including monitoring vital signs, giving medicines and reviewing treatment plans with the patient and loved ones, or to assist a doctor during a medical procedure or surgery.

Social Worker

Social workers provide help and services for needy individuals, families, and communities to cope with a variety of situations, including social, psychological, physical, and emotional challenges. Depending on the town they work with and the needs of that population, those who work may help people access mental health treatment, food assistance, or housing services.

Career Coach

Career advisors help their clients identify, find, and/or create their dream jobs. They help clients achieve their career goals in a variety of ways, including exercises to identify a suitable role or industry, resume and interview training, career goal setting, and accountability support. There are cases where coaches work with clients to improve productivity or leadership, get a raise or promotion, hone communication skills, or achieve other goals beyond the job search.

Human Resources Manager

Human resource managers have responsibility for everything related to people in the company. Depending on the organization and team configuration, managers may be responsible for hiring new employees, administering benefits, leading worker wellness programs, developing people management policies and procedures, and more.

Marketing Manager

A marketing manager oversees work related to promoting a product, service, event, or business. Depending on what they promote, marketing managers may be responsible for a variety of tasks, including conducting market research, developing and managing marketing and advertising campaigns, writing content and marketing materials, managing email accounts and social networks, and the analysis and optimization of campaigns. To understand how to better connect with consumers and drive sales, marketers must gain insight into the minds of target audiences and develop strategies that influence their views and behaviors. Therefore, an empath's ability to understand and interpret the emotions of others will come in handy in this career.

Writer

Being a writer can mean many different things. You could be an author writing a book, a reporter writing a news or featured article, a critic writing a movie or music review, a copywriter writing a script, a content marketer writing articles and blog posts, a publicist writing a press release, a technical writer writing how-to manuals, a UX writer writing web and app content; honestly, the sky is the limit.

Teacher

Teachers have the responsibility of educating students, which may involve developing lecture plans and lessons, creating and supervising educational experiences (such as science experiments or field trips), and offering direct support to students to help them achieve their goals. Teachers can organize extracurricular activities or clubs related to the subjects they teach (for example, a drama teacher can act as director of a school play, while a foreign language teacher can start a conversation club in French for their students).

User Experience Researcher

When a company invests time, money, and various resources in a product or service, it makes sure that what it offers will ultimately serve customers. A product or service should not only bring in the public, but it also has to be simple and easy to use. User experience researchers are responsible for making sure this happens. Researchers collect data through methods such as conducting user interviews or conducting product focus groups and then use that data to drive design decisions and ensure that the final product or service meets customer needs.

Chapter 7

Psychic Astrology and Astro Psychology for Self-Understanding

Now you will have a stronger understanding of what psychic astrology and self-understanding are all about, with empathic listening techniques, feeling desires and not needs, and the true value of empathic abilities. With this chapter, you will be able to open that magnetism and creativity.

Empathic Listening Techniques

For you to use empathic listening, you must patiently listen to what others have to say, even if you disagree. It is important to show acceptance, but not necessarily agreement, simply by nodding or inserting phrases such as "I understand." An empathic listener works hard to prevent the speaker from feeling or becoming defensive. To do this, avoid asking direct questions, arguing about what was said, or arguing about facts. The evidence can be considered later. Now, fully focus on what was said and how the speaker felt.

When the speaker says something that requires additional information, they simply repeat the statement as a question. For example, if the speaker says, "I'm not satisfied with my current position," they can probe further by responding, "You mean you're not satisfied with your current position?" This small amount of encouragement may be enough to prompt the speaker to elaborate. Also, take into account what is not said. Often what a speaker hide is just as important as what they say. Pay attention to your body language. Nonverbal cues, such as tilting their head, walking away, or covering their mouth, can indicate that they are hiding something or that they are uncomfortable.

Empathic Listening Skills

I'll do it with an example:

Ted knocked on Megan's office and simply asked how he could help her. This lowers her defenses, showing his willingness to back her up. He then listens to what she says (and what she doesn't say) and is careful not to interrupt her. It wasn't long before he discovered the problem: Megan had been going through a divorce while she cared for her ailing parents. During their conversation, Ted acts as Megan's mirror. He repeated the main points of what she said so she would know that he understood. During breaks in the conversation, he will transform her comments into questions and ask for more information. Ted also pays attention to Megan's body language. Strangely, the normally confident woman kept her head and eyes lowered throughout the entire conversation. In general, she seems defeated. Starting from there, he begins to help her in the process so that she feels better.

Eye Contact and Lip Reading

When evaluating body language, pay attention to these cues:

* **Pursing lips:** Can indicate disgust, disapproval, or mistrust.
* **Lip biting:** People sometimes bite their lips when they are worried, anxious, or stressed.

- **Covers the mouth:** When people want to hide an emotional reaction, they may cover their mouths to prevent a smile or grimace.
- **Twisting the lips up or down:** Slight changes in the mouth can also subtly indicate how a person is feeling. When the mouth is turned up slightly, it may mean that the person is feeling happy or optimistic. On the other hand, a slightly drooping corner of the mouth can indicate sadness, disapproval, or even a frown.

Eyes

Even when we are asleep, our eyes are constantly moving. Often these are small movements in the eyelids or eyeballs that are difficult to detect. Even so, there are more defined movements to discern what is behind this dynamic. REM (rapid eye movement) sleep is the stage in which the eyes move the fastest.

If the eyes move up and to the right, the brain's memory mechanisms may have been activated. Movement means to evoke a past event or situation. On the contrary, if they move up and to the left, it is likely that creative functions related to the visual domain have been activated. This movement usually occurs when we capture an image that surprises us.

Downward-looking eyes indicate that we have entered the process of introspection. If the gaze is to the left, it must be because some situation or some information is being calculated. If it moves to the right, it indicates that memory processes related to bodily sensations are taking place.

Feel the Desires and Not the Needs

When you see yourself and others, you have to see and feel the desires, not the needs, because many times, these are ephemeral. Desires can be something you want to possess, and ironically, they can become a need.

What a Psychic Empath Can Bring to the World

When awake, the empath can see the symbolism in the situation. We can observe what happens in our bodies, our businesses, and the world and understand the deeper implications. This bird's-eye view allows us to detach ourselves from the minutiae of the situation and address the real issues that need attention.

We Make a Difference by Being Visionary Leaders

When we take responsibility for our gifts (I like to call them superpowers) and stand up for our future, we bring much-needed harmony to the world. Sometimes we feel that our ability to see the good in others makes us vulnerable. However, this powerful talent, when used correctly, is a rare and useful tool. If you're having trouble being taken advantage of, consider developing your empathy skills.

Intuition

"Everyone has insights, but empathic insight is very real." —Colette Davenport

Dr. Caroline Myss, in her book *The Anatomy of the Mind*, says that the solar plexus chakra (the navel chakra) is the power center that maintains our self-esteem and self-confidence. It incorporates our "survival instincts," the senses that protect us when we are in physical danger and alert us to negative energy and other people's actions. When we ignore our intuition, we violate this energy. Our ability to be guided by our intuition requires that we have a strong sense of self-respect.

Meese continued: "Equally important is the role of self-esteem in healing and maintaining a healthy body."

So, when we lack self-esteem and self-love, our relationships lack certainty, our intuition fails, and our lives feel out of our control. Mastering our energy and emotions, along with confidence and self-esteem, are some of the keys to being an empath.

Psychic Abilities

This is where I get a little weird, but if you're like me, it's totally normal. Empaths are not only emotionally gifted but psychologically tuned in as well. These blows can come in a variety of forms, similar to intuition. What's different about this though, is that we can be hundreds of miles away from someone and still feel what's going on.

Well, this is what I call my people. On some level, you already know that you have the power to heal yourself and others, but have you fully accepted this, or are you still trying to be normal? For years, I tried to numb myself and be a "normal" person.

If you're like me, some of this may resonate: I used to feel helpless, hopeless, and out of control. I have struggled with self-esteem for much of my life. For years, I was confused and frustrated. Then I learned to use empathic abilities.

- **Vision:** I see the deepest wounds (at the soul level) as the root of my disease.
- **Intuition:** I stopped tolerating self-sabotage and built self-esteem and self-confidence.
- **Psychic abilities:** I accepted what made me special and stopped trying to fit in.
- **Being:** I learned to love myself unconditionally and allow others to be who they are. I gave up trying to control everything.
- **The power of healing:** I recognize our amazing and unique AF power. I used mine to heal my heart and now to transform my body.
- **Creativity:** I changed the focus of my life's work to serve my empathy.

The True Value of Your Empathic Abilities

When we're going through tough times, battling burnout, or having a hard time finding joy at work, empathy can be a powerful antidote, leading to positive experiences both individually and as a team. A new Catalyst study of 889 employees found that empathy has some significant constructive effects:

- **Innovation.** When people reported that their leaders were empathic, they were more likely to report that they could innovate: sixty-one percent of employees, compared to just thirteen percent of empathic leaders.
- **Promise.** Seventy-six percent of those who experienced empathy from leaders were committed, compared to thirty-two percent of those who experienced less empathy.
- **Booking.** Fifty-seven percent of white women and sixty-two percent of women of color said they were less likely to consider leaving a company when they felt the company respected and valued their living environment. However, only fourteen percent of white women and thirty percent of women of color, respectively, said they were less likely to consider leaving when they didn't feel that level of value or respect for their living environment.
- **Tolerance.** Fifty percent of those with empathic leaders say their workplace is inclusive, compared to just seventeen percent who lack empathic leadership.
- **Working life.** When people feel their leaders are more empathetic, eighty-six percent report being able to cope with the demands of work and life, juggling personal, family, and work obligations. Instead, sixty percent felt less empathy.

Your Empathy Is How Many People Identify with You

Being an empathic person means that you have a wonderful gift. You get a sense of how people, situations, circumstances, and behavior are feeling without specific prompting or feedback. As an empath, you enjoy powerful inner wisdom that gives you great potential for powerful transformation. There's a little voice inside of you, and the more you listen to it, the louder it gets. As an empath, some people may make derogatory comments or gestures toward you. This is because they do not understand what it is to be an empath since they cannot feel or perceive it. They are closed. However, I am a firm believer that we are all capable of developing some kind of empathic intuition if we really want to.

Even if, after reading this, you don't feel like you're an empath, chances are you can empathize with other people too, but you haven't realized when it's happening. This is completely understandable, as the lack of a clear line between the physical and immaterial worlds can fool even the most skilled empaths. Ultimately, we all belong to different ratios of rippling energy. With practice, even the most enthusiastic non-empath will have to admit that they can sense another person's energy as soon as they start listening.

Empathy Can Solve Many Situations if You Are Creative Enough

As an empath, you offer an oasis of calm and comfort to those you come in contact with. Even if you feel tired, moody, or broken at times, take heart from the tremendous positivity and support you bring to other people in your life. Take steps to rejuvenate yourself regularly. Also, be aware of your own limitations. Learn to be your best friend because a nurturing soul is a generous soul. And more importantly, because you deserve it.

The Empathic Counselor

You will find that, as an empath, you tend to sit on the sidelines and find it difficult to hide your emotions. Honesty and integrity are extremely important to empathy. You find it impossible to pretend you like something or find something interesting that doesn't resonate with you. Also, your gestures are likely to give you away. Empaths act from an honest point of view. That means it's almost impossible to want to be someone you're not. You are what people see. Empaths have the uncanny ability to spot liars. They instinctively feel it. As an empath, you have a strong intuitive voice that can tell you when things are right or wrong. Somehow you figured it out.

You are picky about the people you spend time with. Empathic people often have only a small group of trusted friends with whom they feel comfortable. Empaths have an instinctive ability to avoid toxic people, possibly because they can feel a vortex of energy closing in on them. As an empath, your life is likely to be unconsciously influenced by the desires, thoughts, and emotions of others. This can cause you to act outside of your true nature. You subconsciously shape your behavior to match that of those around you. You probably remember many times when you wondered why you behaved in a way that was completely contrary to your principles. Usually, you absorb the energy of the person influencing you and don't clearly review your beliefs until you're alone again. Alone time is very important for empathy, especially when spent in nature. Empaths tend to be very happy in their own skin because it gives them a chance to recalibrate and stay put without the influence of another person's energy.

The Personality That Gives It All

Empaths are prone to emotional instability due to their sensitivity to experiencing the emotions of others. Let's face it, people tend to emit more negativity than positivity. Emotional instability can cause the empath to suppress the pain they are experiencing, which can lead to substance abuse and eating disorders. The absorption of negative energy often causes the empath to suffer from anxiety-related digestive disorders.

An empathic person needs to realize that they are empathic, not an "over-sensitive" person who lives a life surrounded by people who do not "get" their life. That moment of discovery can be life-changing, strengthening empathy to learn how to protect and ground yourself. Empathy is often very sensitive to changes in weather and air pressure. That heavy, muddy feeling like a storm is coming? It's almost as if the air was filled with an invisible layer of lead. Of the five senses (sight, hearing, touch, smell, taste), touch tends to be the strongest. Empathy is tactile and often comes dressed in comfort rather than charm. Restrictive clothing goes against comfort, the need for freedom, and mobility. Empathic people prefer soft and natural fabrics.

Empaths use intuition as their primary language. They often have a feeling that certain things are going to happen a certain way. Intuitively, empathy can help you understand people's emotions before they say or do something. When empathic people feel disaster coming on, listen to them! Have you ever had the feeling that something is not going according to plan? Or do you have that feeling that a friend will let you down at the last moment? Or do you turn around and look directly at a complete stranger whose eyes are locked on yours? That's your intuition at work.

Empathic people often find it difficult to ensure lasting peace in close relationships. This is because it feels like your energy and freedom are being controlled by you. This manifests due to an overwhelming need to spend time alone. This is also due to the empath's tendency to transform into the partner's energy field. This means that they can lose and be deprived of their true selves. Also, empaths often end up giving more than they can afford in the long run. Your love of helping and connecting with others creates a long list of debits when you run out of energy to maintain the status quo.

In intimate relationships, the value of alone time and freedom can be difficult to maintain. Too complex for a relationship. Thus, the empath ends up being single most of the time. One advantage that can help an empath in this situation is their ability to be happy on their own.

Likewise, when empaths fall in love, it is often with another empath. When they are safe enough in their respective surroundings, empaths can form close and caring relationships. Furthermore, they operate on mutual respect for the needs of others and are focused on a deep sense of trust.

Music Appreciation

Music has been called a "universal language," the language of emotion, but people vary greatly in their emotional fluidity. When we listen to music, like when listening to a desperate, angry, or elated friend, some of us seem to be more emotional than others. One listener couldn't help but cringe at a certain Billie Holiday song, accepting her tragedy sympathetically and perhaps with a bit of sentiment, while another was just frozen. A person can be inspired by an upbeat pop song while you may be just bored. Perhaps these differences are not simply a product of musical taste—is the tendency to contemplate and vicariously experience the emotional content of music related to how well someone is generally attuned to the emotions of others in everyday life?

Expressiveness

Empaths are constantly tired while absorbing the emotions of others. They are prone to eating disorders, self-harm, and substance abuse. These behaviors are often used to help ease the emotional pain experienced by some empaths. It is for these reasons that it is crucial to know how to take care of yourself and find balance in your life. Here are some simple steps you can take regularly to help keep you grounded and healthy.

Deep Breathing

Deep breathing helps us relax. It nourishes the body and collaborates to detoxify us by stimulating the lymphatic system. Deep breathing will help you stay calm and find relief when fatigue threatens to overwhelm you.

Meditation

Meditation, as you saw before, serves to clear emotional clutter and re-align with peace. Get in the habit of meditating for a few minutes at least once a day. Meditation serves to clear mental clutter, plus it helps you tune in to restorative energies.

Water

The adult human body is made up of approximately sixty percent water. This is essential to maintain internal and external homeostasis. You drink it to clean the inside and detoxify. Bathe in it to clear negative energy. If you shower, you can put a few tablespoons of rock salt in the water. Salt has a purifying effect and helps you eliminate negative energy. It also helps soothe tired muscles. If you shower instead of bathing, mix a few pinches of salt with oil and a few drops of your favorite essential oil. Rub it on your skin and wash it off. It not only cleanses you but also leaves you with silky smooth skin. Lavender, rose, and chamomile essential oils are relaxing and smell great.

Nature

Like I said before, get some time outside, especially when the sun is shining and warming you gently, in the mornings or at sunset, to help increase your UV levels. If it's hot enough, walk barefoot and benefit from the earth's negative ions to help rebalance your energy. Awaken all your senses. Listen to the call of nature, fill the nasal cavity with the fragrance of nature, feel the touch of nature and skin, marvel at the vibrant colors of nature, and reap the fruits of nature.

Gratitude

Whether it's prayer or gratitude, take a moment to be thankful for each day of your life. Gratitude can improve physical and mental health and help restore energy levels. Gratitude also tunes your subconscious mind to look for the positive. The more positives you attract, the more positives you can give.

Sympathy

Empathy means that you see other people's emotions as your own. For example, if the people around you are very angry, you may start to feel angry yourself, even if you don't have an immediate reason to feel that way. Observing another person's emotional state activates parts of the neural network involved in processing that same state, be it disgust, touch, or pain.

Perceptive Healer

The therapist has the ability to "see" the whole of a person, not the sum of their parts. The job of a therapist is to help remove obstacles to personal growth. It is now an accepted fact that human beings are electromagnetic beings. All diseases are caused by lowering the body's frequency below what is necessary to maintain homeostasis. By raising the frequency and tuning the different bodies, all the fields become coherent. That is health.

Energy healing has been around forever and is one of the oldest healing techniques you can use to keep your body in a state of balance and health. The ancients were aware of the psychological and physical effects we experience on our own minds, the minds of other people, and the unseen forces "out there." Alternative energy therapy includes these mental and spiritual domains, as well as the physical domains.

Born Leaders

Empathic leadership is the art of leadership that understands, identifies with, and shares the experiences of others. It is the ability to put yourself in someone else's shoes and see the world through their eyes. It's being able to understand what it's like to be a member of an underrepresented team in leadership and understand their unique struggles and obstacles. They can see the big picture and long game and use that view to help others see it too.

It is about understanding the experiences of others. It's about knowing how others think, feel, and behave, and then communicating effectively with them in a way that brings out great potential. It's about putting yourself in their shoes and thinking about them instead of just talking about them. This allows you to connect with them on a deeper level, which naturally increases empathy, compassion, and connection. It is not easy to be a great leader when you are an empathic leader. At the best of times, you're always on the edge, constantly looking for clues as to how people are really feeling and worrying about how your decisions will affect them.

Many Interesting Friends

Since you have the gift of filtering and putting into action that intuition where you have good people by your side and you stay away from the toxic ones or those who do you no good, that is why you have many interesting friends and people of value who are genuine.

Magnetism

Empaths have a charm that unites people. It's like they have a sign tattooed on their forehead that says, "Come and tell me your deepest, darkest secret." Does this happen to you? Do you end up hearing problems from complete strangers? It's like an invisible thread that draws people to you. Similarly, empaths get along with a wide variety of people from all walks of life. This is because they can tune in to the energy of the person they are communicating with.

Strong Links

As I said before, you can have strong ties with people because your filter will help you attract the best. In addition, that empathy and heart that you have will help you have great connections that the Universe sends you.

Creativity

Creativity is a gift that enhances and enriches your life. Your creative talents are an asset that can bring joy, insight, and innovation that could not be achieved otherwise. You will use your imagination to be creative, but your psychic abilities are the true engine of this wonderful aspect of your life

Can You Learn to Channel Your Psychic Abilities into Your Creativity?

Psychic ability rarely gets the credit it deserves as an element of creativity. However, this is an important aspect to recognize. This ability is enhanced in some people, and if you are one of these gifted people, it is sometimes misunderstood.

Why Is the Psychic Ability an Attribute to Creativity?

The psyche is defined as the ability of the soul to capture information beyond the limitations of our physical senses. Creativity fits this definition and is therefore fueled by psychic abilities. However, the ability of each individual's consciousness (also known as soul) to open up and receive cosmic energy is individual. Creative people are often seen as geniuses by others because they come up with new, simple, and sometimes revolutionary ideas or inventions. It simplifies complexities and solutions that are sometimes completely overlooked.

Déjà Vu

Déjà vu is a common intuitive experience that many of us have experienced. The expression is of French origin and means "already seen." When it happens, it seems to trigger our memories of places we've been, people we've met, or actions we've taken. This is a signal to pay special attention to what is going on, perhaps to take a specific course in an area or to complete something that has not yet been completed. Some of the theories to explain *déjà vu* are dream memories, precognition, coincidental accumulation of events, and even past life experiences in which we rekindle old alliances. What matters is that it brings us closer to the mystery. It is an offering, an opportunity to acquire additional knowledge about ourselves and about others.

Some cases fail when the rules are bent, and mystery prevails. Glamorous moments. These are *déjà vu*. They can happen anywhere, with anyone. Your real estate agent can show you a home that feels so familiar and appropriate that you'll immediately know it's yours. Or maybe you're in a restaurant and feel an inexplicable bond with a woman sitting at a table in the back corner. Don't let these possibilities pass you by. There's no way to predict where each might go or what it will teach you. Having the courage to take risks and act in tune, having faith in what is not yet visible, will make the experience your own.

Before the Conclusion

Empaths are highly advanced souls who are here for a different and brilliant purpose. If anything, we should focus on the innate strength, amazing resourcefulness, and resilience that empaths can withstand after particularly severe karmic waves. Among what you can do to help others and that your gift is part of those around you, you have the following choices:

You Become a Beacon of Light and Fun

When an empath decides to stop absorbing as a way to help others, they take control of their energy field and begin to channel higher states of consciousness. The key is to be intense at the moment. Forget introversion and extroversion; once you flip the mirror that people cast by protecting your energy field, you immediately raise the bar and become your own source of energy. Yes, that's right, you actually completely transcend all energy exchanges and become the conduit directly from the source to the human path. You have to experience it to feel the thrill.

You Can Communicate with the Entire Human Race Telepathically

Through your inner knowing, you can telepathically speak to people about their inner wealth or higher truths. Trust me, you are that smart. This is probably why you seem confusing and strange to people who are used to repeating dull conversations. When you meet someone who is living the truth but juggling so many things at the same time (a person who recognizes their own timeline and not simultaneously), you can see why empathic communication can be stressful.

Plant Love Through Eye Contact

The downside of a narcissistic relationship is that it erodes the empath's confidence in spreading the love that they are capable of spreading, and many empaths suffer from this in the early stages. Simply by increasing your frequency when you walk down the street, you can catch the attention of people passing by and "implant" them all with that frequency (or maybe even make their day). Sounds like a scene from a sci-fi movie, doesn't it? But as a highly sensitive energetic being, you will know how this works.

Conclusion

Connecting with this gift that you possess is one of the greatest favors you can do to yourself and the universe because not only you will begin to flow and feel better, but you will also be able to transcend and help others, read their auras, and help them to clear emotions. You will always know how to walk a path where you feel comfortable.

Intuition, that power, the third eye looking out for you, will help you to channel many energies, to open up the deep love you have and share it with others, and that leadership that is sometimes hidden emerges forcefully for others. You have that power; you were born with a developed faculty that most humans do not have, do not take it as a burden when it is actually a gift from the Universe. If you got here, I appreciate your reading. I hope my knowledge has helped you to better understand everything you are, I appreciate that you have chosen this book, and I hope you can take a moment to leave a review.

Made in United States
Troutdale, OR
09/26/2023

13203098R00049